Decadent SHAKES

MILKSHAKES WITH MORE

We dedicate this book
to all those who have
shared a smile, a laugh
or a memory with us
along the way!

Enjoy and love life,
Matt, Sarah and Brendo.

MATTHEW, SARAH & BRENDAN AOUAD

Decadent
SHAKES
MILKSHAKES WITH MORE

CONTENTS

Introduction	6
Notes About Safety	9
Decorating Your Glass	11
Fruity Mania	13
Chocolate Mania	27
Super Sweet	59
Crazy Cool	83
Glossary Of Treats	102
Index	106
Acknowledgements	109
Author Bio	109

INTRODUCTION

The Vogue Café has been in our family since 2012 with each sibling bringing their own unique story and experience to the cafe. We have been able to create a Decadent Shake bar away from the hustle and bustle of the busy shops and give our customers a place to call home.

The shakes we design and make have a lot of love in them, as friends and family work together to build these intriguing and deliciously decadent creations.

Growing up we were always competitive siblings. When we took over the family café in 2012 we started holding 'Thursday night experiments' where we would play around with tastes, textures, colors, shapes – anything you could think of. Apart from having a crazy amount of fun, these sessions were also where we founded some of our most decadent and delicious shake creations.

Whenever we create specials, it is Sarah and Matt that are all about the taste, while Brendan is always on top of aesthetic of the design. This has led to some of our craziest looking shakes, like the Double Decker, which includes a waffle AND a waffle cone – filled with mint chocolate and topped with caramels.

Or the Infamous Nutella Milkshake, which we created in 2013, and which was an instant hit, drawing chocolate fiends from every corner of the world to come and indulge in this unique, mind blowing shake.

The decadent shakes that you find in this book are the end result of beloved childhood memories, things that we as kids loved to indulge in (sometimes too much!).

Choosing just 40 shakes wasn't an easy task, but after countless hours sorting through the archives of our favorite concoctions, we landed on what you have before you, 40 of our most decadent creations, including the now famous (and infamous!) Nutella Milkshake, which continues to blow the minds and taste buds of everyone who dares to indulge.

There is something for every taste, even between the three of us we have really different tastes. Matt's favorite is the Salty Knickers – a mouth watering combination of pretzels and Snickersl Sarah raves about Billy Bonka – a insane combination of waffles, Snickers, Oreos, pretzels and peanut butter; and Brendan's a loyal sucker for Nutella, sour worms and Licorice, so the Infamous Nutella Milkshake is his go to.

We hope these shakes also serve as a source of inspiration for your own foodie creativity. They're a shining symbol of the importance of fun and not taking life too seriously. Have fun at home, go on a shopping frenzy and bring back an array of treats –sweet and savory – snacks, cake mix, candies, ice creams; you name it and just have a go!

Happy Shaking!

NOTES ABOUT SAFETY

Safety disclaimer: DO NOT attempt to eat off the chocolate or decorations that are melted onto the rim of the glass as the glass may crack when bitten.

If you must have the chocolate and decorations it is best to use a spoon to scrape off the melted chocolate.

With all milk based drinks, you can easily substitute milk for soy milk or any other products, however we do recommended adding 10 per cent more liquid, especially if you remove the ice cream, as the drink does not thicken up as much!

DECORATING YOUR GLASS

The effect of the chocolate rimmed glass is best achieved using bain marie of chocolate. Being home shake enthusiasts we don't expect you to have a bain marie to use, so you can grab Belgian milk chocolate and Belgian dark chocolate buds from your local supermarket and melt them in a pot on the stove. A good amount of chocolate for a chocolate rim is about 200g (7oz).

CHOCOLATE RIM

Once the chocolate buds have been melted, dip the rim of the glass into the chocolate about 1cm (1/2 in) deep. Smoothly, roll the glass around so that all sides are covered. Place the glass in the fridge and let stand for at least 5 minutes.

SUGAR RIM

The effect of the sugar rim is achieved by covering the rim of the glass with the juice of a slice of lemon or lime. Cover the rim with the juice 3–4 times and then quickly and evenly dip the rim of the glass into a cup of sugar and leave the glass to set in the fridge for a minimum of 20 minutes.

WHIPPED CREAM

To add flavor, if you own a whipped cream cannister, add flavored syrups. At the cafe we use vanilla syrup for flavors (unless stated otherwise) however adding chocolate syrup turns the cream chocolate color or strawberry would turn the cream red. Keep this in mind if you want to crate your own Decadent Shakes for an added layer of color!

EXTRA ADDITIONS

To add sprinkles, coconut or anything other glass decorations, wait one minute after dipping the glass into the chocolate, and dip the glass into the sprinkles, coconut, or anything else you'd like to rim the glass and roll the glass around evenly coat the rim. Leave the glass in the fridge to set for a minimum of 30 minutes.

FRUITY MANIA

- PEACH AS BRO
- PASH ME
- PEACHY MANGO
- CHAINANA
- MAN-GO-CRAZY
- PINA COLADA
- MIXED BERRY SMOOTHIE

Fruity Fun

PEACH AS BRO

SHAKE INGREDIENTS

- 375g (13oz) frozen peaches
- 8 frozen strawberries
- 200ml (7fl oz) passionfruit quencher
- 4 tsp strawberry syrup
- 4 tsp peach syrup

For presentation
- 1 glass with sugar rim
- 1 long straw
- 1 lemon
- 1 mint sprig
- 125g (4oz) frozen mixed berries

Method
› Place all the ingredients in a blender and mix until well combined. While the ingredients are blending, cut the lemon in half and start slicing into thin moon slices.

Decorate
› Before pouring the mixture into the glass, create a sugar rim along the top of your glass (see page 13).
› Pour the blended mixture into the glass, until it reaches half way up to the rim.
› Place the straw on the inside right hand side of the jar and place the 3 lemon slices on the left hand side of straw, fanning them out as you slide them in.
› Place the mint sprig in front of the straw and cover the remainder of the drink with frozen mixed berries.
› Serve immediately and enjoy!

PASH ME

SHAKE INGREDIENTS

- handful fresh mint leaves
- 400ml (14fl oz) white peach and passionfruit quencher
- handful of frozen fruits (mixed berries and peach)

For presentation:
- 1 glass with sugar rim
- 1 long straw
- 1 passionfruit (cut in half)
- 3 slices lemon
- 3 slices lime
- ice cubes

Method:

› Before pouring the mixture into the glass, create a sugar rim along the top of your glass (see page 13).
› Tear off 5 mint leaves and place them into the glass with the ice cubes.
› Place your lemon and lime slices and frozen fruit into the glass.
› Fill the glass to the rim with white peach and passionfruit quencher.
› Place a straw on the right side of the glass.

Decorate:

› Place half of the sliced passionfruit on top of the glass, bottom side up.
› Scoop the passionfruit pulp from the unused half onto the top of the drink to cover.
› Spread the remaining mint leaves around the passionfruit to create a flower.
› Serve immediately and enjoy!

TIP! To make this quencher a frappe, just add ice and blend!

Super Sweet

Fruity Fun

PEACHY MANGO

SHAKE INGREDIENTS

- 7 cubes frozen mango
- 450g (15oz) diced frozen peaches
- 200ml (7fl oz) pineapple juice
- 2tbsp peach syrup

For presentation:
- 1 glass with sugar rim
- 1 long straw
- 250g (4oz) frozen mixed berries
- 1 lime, sliced
- 1 mint sprig

Method:
> Place all the ingredients in a blender jug and mix until well combined. While the ingredients are blending, slice the lime into thin slices.

Decorate:
> Before pouring the mixture into the glass, create a sugar rim along the top of your glass (see page 13).
> Pour the blended mixture into the glass until it reaches the rim.
> Place the straw on the right side of the glass and place three slices of lime on the left of the straw fanning out and away from the straw. Place the mint sprig in front of straw and use mixed berries to cover the top of the rest of the drink.
> Serve immediately and enjoy!

CHAINANA

SHAKE INGREDIENTS

- 1/2 banana
- 3 scoops vanilla ice cream
- 1 tbsp organic chai powder
- 200ml (7fl oz) milk
- 1 tsp honey

For presentation:
- 1 chocolate rimmed glass
- 1 long straw
- whipped cream
- 4 banana candies
- 1 cube Jersey Caramels
- 4 orange m&m's
- 1 cinnamon stick

Method:
- Place all of the shake ingredients in a blender and mix until well combined.
- While the ingredients are blending, slice up the Jersey Caramels into four pieces and tear the cinnamon stick into long thin pieces.

Decorate:
- Before pouring the mixture into the glass, create a chocolate rim around the top of the glass (see page 13).
- Pour in the blended mixture until it reaches halfway up the glass.
- Place a straw in middle of the jar and fill the remainder of the jar with whipped cream.
- Place the banana candies around the straw.
- Slide the Jersey Caramels in between the banana candies and add one m&m in front of each jersey
- Sprinkle the cinnamon stick pieces around the straw.
- Serve immediately and enjoy!

Fruity Fun
23

Fruity Fun
24

MAN-GO-CRAZY

SHAKE INGREDIENTS

- 6 cubes frozen mango
- 2 mini Crunchie chocolate bars
- 250g (8oz) caramel popcorn
- 1 pump chocolate syrup
- 1 pump caramel syrup
- 2 scoops vanilla ice cream
- 200ml (7fl oz) milk

For presentation:
- 1 chocolate rimmed glass
- 1 long straw
- 1 waffle basket
- 2 scoops vanilla ice cream
- melting chocolate
- 1 cinnamon donut
- 2 mini Crunchie chocolate bars
- 125g (4oz) caramel popcorn
- 1 syrup syringe
- 1 tsp caramel syrup

Method:

> Place all of the shake ingredients in a blender and mix until well combined.
> While the ingredients are blending, create a hole in the left/middle side of the waffle basket and crush the Crunchie into fine pieces.

Decorate:

> Before pouring the mixture into the glass, create a chocolate rim around the top of the glass (see page 13).
> Pour in the blended mixture until it reaches halfway up the glass.
> Place a straw through the hole in the waffle basket and place 2 scoops of ice cream into the basket.
> Melt the melting chocolate as per the directions on the packet. Dip one side of the donut into the melted chocolate and then dip the donut into the crushed up Crunchie.
> Once the donut has dried, place it over the straw.
> Scatter the caramel popcorn on top of the ice cream.
> Fill syringe with caramel syrup and place on right side of donut.
> Drizzle the remaining melted chocolate and crushed Crunchie over the caramel popcorn.
> Serve immediately and enjoy!

PINA COLADA

SHAKE INGREDIENTS

- 125g (4oz) diced frozen pineapple pieces
- 200ml (7fl oz) pineapple juice
- 5 ice cubes
- 1 1/2 heaped tbsp shredded coconut

For Presentation:
- 1 chocolate rimmed glass
- 1 long straw
- brown sugar
- shredded coconut
- 1 kiwi fruit, sliced
- 1 stem fresh mint
- 2 yellow Jubes
- 1 mini chocolate flake bar

Method:
› Place all the shake ingredients in a blender and mix until well combined.
› While the ingredients are spinning, slice the kiwi into thin slices.

Decorate:
› Before pouring the mixture into the glass, create a chocolate rim around the top of the glass (see page 13).
› Pour the ingredients into the glass until it reaches the rim.
› Place the straw at the back of the glass leaning towards the right and fill the rest of the glass with shredded coconut. Place the stem of mint in the glass on the left side of straw.
› Place the sliced kiwi fruit slightly in front of the straw, so that it covers the mint.
› Add in the yellow Jubes, placing them in front of the mint.
› Finish the drink by breaking up the flake chocolate bar and sprinkling it over the drink.
› Serve immediately and enjoy!

Fruity Fun
27

Fruity Fun
28

MIXED BERRY SMOOTHIE

SHAKE INGREDIENTS

- 125g (4oz) frozen mixed berries
- 3 scoops vanilla ice cream

For presentation:
- 1 chocolate rimmed glass
- 1 long straw
- handful desiccated coconut
- 1 stem of fresh mint leaves

- 200ml (7fl oz) milk
- 1 teaspoon strawberry syrup

- red and purple mini jelly lollies
- 2 jelly mint leaves
- 2 chocolate Pocky Sticks
- 1 small waffle cone, with chocolate and coconut rim.

Method:
› Place all the shake ingredients in a blender and mix until well combined.

Decorate:
› Before pouring the mixture into the glass, create a chocolate rim around the top of the glass (see page 13).
› Once the chocolate rim is almost dry, layer on the desiccated coconut around the rim.
› Pour the ingredients into the glass until it reaches the rim.
› Cover the top of the mixture with the remaining desiccated coconut.
› Cut a hole in the base of the waffle cone and place the cone at the back of the glass.
› Weave the straw through the cone and into the shake.
› Remove the mint leaves from the stem and place the leaves in the waffle cone.
› Place the red and purple mini jelly lollies around the rim of the glass, alternating in color.
› Place the 2 jelly mint leaves in front of the waffle cone.
› Place the two chocolate Pocky Sticks at the back of the cone.
› Serve immediately and enjoy!

CHOCOLATE MANIA

- CRUNCHIE KISSES
- CHOCOLATE MILKSHAKE
- MALT MY HEART
- MOCHA MADNESS
- SALTY KNICKERS
- MAGIC DOODLE
- DOUBLE DECKER
- MC'MAZING
- ICED CHOCOLATE
- BUENO MARS
- JENGA
- TWERK IT
- COACHELLA
- BILLY BONKA

Chocolate Mania

CRUNCHIE KISSES

SHAKE INGREDIENTS

- 2 small Crunchie chocolate bars
- 3 fresh strawberries
- 1 Kinder Bueno stick
- 200ml (7fl oz) milk
- 1 tbsp vanilla custard
- 1 Kinder egg
- 7 ice cubes

For presentation:
- 1 chocolate covered glass
- 1 long straw
- half cinnamon donut
- Persian fairy floss
- 2 Pocky Sticks
- 1 mini Crunchie chocolate bars
- 2 small red jelly frogs
- 4 Ovalteenies
- sprinkles
- 1 Kinder chocolate stick
- 1/2 Kinder Bueno chocolate stick
- whipped cream, to fill
- sprinkles

Method:
> Place all of the shake ingredients into a blender and mix until well combined.

Decorate:
> Before pouring the mixture into the glass, create a chocolate rim around the top of the glass (see page 13).

> Pour the blended mixture into the glass until it reaches the bottom of the rim.

> Place the straw at the back in the middle of glass. Fill the remainder of the jar with whipped cream.

> Place the half cinnamon donut in front of the straw to the left side of the glass, hooking it over the side of the glass.

> Place 2 red jelly frogs in front of the donut so that the frogs are on the edge of the glass.

> Place 3 Pocky Sticks on the right hand side of straw and place the Kinder stick and Kinder Bueno in front of the Pocky Sticks.

> Cut the small Crunchie in half and place both halves on the right hand side of the glass.

> Put a small amount of whipped cream on top of the donut and then top with the Persian fairy floss.

> Top the fairy floss with a sprinkling of Ovalteenies and sprinkles.

> Serve immediately and enjoy!

CHOCOLATE MILKSHAKE

SHAKE INGREDIENTS

- 3 pumps chocolate syrup
- 2 scoops vanilla ice cream
- 300ml (10fl oz) milk

For presentation:
- 1 chocolate rimmed glass
- 1 long straw
- 1 jelly snake
- Rice Bubbles
- colored popcorn

Method:
› Place all ingredients in a blender and mix until well combined.

Decorate:
› Before pouring the mixture into the glass, create a chocolate rim around the top of the glass (see page 13).
› Pour the blended mixture into the glass until it reaches the rim of the glass.
› Scatter the Rice Bubbles over the shake until it is entirely covered.
› Place a straw on right side of milkshake.
› Wrap a jelly snake around the straw and place colored popcorn on top of the Rice Bubbles until the glass is completely covered.

TIP: Repeat this recipe for other classic milkshake flavors such like slimy lime, super strawberry, nana banana, crazy caramel and very cool vanilla.

Chocolate Mania

Chocolate Mania

MALT MY HEART

SHAKE INGREDIENTS

- 1 ½ tbsp malt
- 3 pumps chocolate syrup
- 2 scoops vanilla ice cream
- 200ml (7fl oz) milk
- 2 mini chocolate Flake bars

For presentation:
- 1 chocolate rimmed glass
- 1 long straw
- 3 Maltesers chocolate
- 8 m&m's
- whipped cream
- 1 chocolate Flake bar, crushed

Method:
› Place all the ingredients into a blender and mix until well combined.
› While milkshake is blending, chop the Maltesers into halves and set aside for decorating. Crush up the chocolate flake bar and set aside.

Decorate:
› Before pouring the mixture into the glass, create a chocolate rim around the top of the glass (see page 13).
› Pour the blended mixture into the glass until it reaches the rim.
› Place the Maltesers around the edge of the jar leaving a small gap in between.
› Place the m&m's in between the Maltesers and cover them with whipped cream with the crushed chocolate Flake pieces.
› Serve immediately and enjoy!

MOCHA MADNESS

SHAKE INGREDIENTS

- 1 tsp coffee
- 3 pumps chocolate syrup
- 2 scoops vanilla ice cream
- 250ml (8fl oz) milk

For presentation:
- 1 chocolate rimmed glass
- 1 long straw
- whipped cream
- 125g (4oz) mixed m&m's
- 1 chocolate Flake bar

Method:
› Place all the ingredients in a blender and mix until well combined.
› While the ingredients are mixing, crush up the flake and add to your chocolate rimmed glass at set aside.

Decorate:
› Before pouring the mixture into the glass, create a chocolate rim around the top of the glass (see page 13).
› Pour the blended mixture into the glass until it reaches the bottom of the rim.
› Place straw in the middle and fill the remainder with whipped cream.
› Cover the cream in the m&m's .
› Serve immediately and enjoy!

Chocolate Mania

Chocolate
Mania
40

SALTY KNICKERS

SHAKE INGREDIENTS

- 250g (8oz) salted pretzels
- 4 mini Snickers bars
- 1 tbsp smooth peanut butter
- 2 pumps caramel syrup
- 1 pump chocolate syrup
- 2 scoops vanilla ice cream
- 200ml (7fl oz) milk

For presentation:
- 1 chocolate rimmed glass
- 1 long straw
- whipped cream
- chocolate powder, to sprinkle
- 2 salted pretzels
- 1 mini Snickers bars
- 60g (2oz) peanut granules

Method:
- Place all the ingredients in a blender and mix until well combined.
- While the mixture is blending, slice the Snickers bars and set aside for decorating.

Decorate:
- Before pouring the mixture into the glass, create a chocolate rim around the top of the glass (see page 13).
- Pour in the blended mixture until it reaches the bottom of the rim.
- Place a straw in the middle, back of the glass and create a mini tower with whipped cream.
- Dust chocolate powder over the whipped cream and place two pretzels upside down in front of straw. Place two pieces of the sliced Snickers bar in front of one pretzel, and two in front of the other pretzel.
- Sprinkle peanut granules over the shake to serve.
- Serve immediately and enjoy!

MAGIC DOODLE

SHAKE INGREDIENTS

- 2 mini Crunchie bars
- 3 Oreo biscuits
- 1 tbsp Nutella
- 1 tsp caramel syrup
- 8 ice cubes
- 100ml (3fl oz) milk

For presentation:
- 1 chocolate rimmed glass
- 1 long straw
- 1 Oreo cookie
- 3 Pocky sticks
- 1 small packet of Mamee noodles
- handful of mini m&m's
- 2 mini red frogs

Method:

› Place all the ingredients in a blender and mix until well combined.
› While the mixture is blending, slice the Snickers bars and set aside for decorating.

Decorate:

› Before pouring the mixture into the glass, create a chocolate rim around the top of the glass (see page 13).
› Pour in the blended mixture until it reaches the bottom of the rim.
› Place a straw in the middle, back of the glass and create a mini tower with whipped cream.
› Place the Pocky sticks at the back of the glass to the right of the straw.
› Break up the Mamee noodles lengthways and place three strips of noodles in front of the straw.
› Place the red frogs on the edge of the jar, in front of the noodles and then cover the remaining cream with mini m&m's to serve.
› Serve immediately and enjoy!

Chocolate Mania

43

Chocolate
Mania

DOUBLE DECKER

SHAKE INGREDIENTS

- 1 mint Golden Gaytime ice cream
- 2 mini Crunchie chocolate bars
- 1 tbsp Nutella
- 1 pump caramel syrup
- 1 pump chocolate syrup
- 2 scoops vanilla ice cream
- 200ml (7fl oz) milk

For presentation:
- 1 chocolate rimmed glass
- 1 long straw
- drizzle chocolate syrup
- 1 large waffle cone
- melting chocolate
- 1 scoop vanilla ice cream
- whipped cream
- 1 waffle basket
- half block mint chocolate
- 5 chocolate chips
- 2 toffees
- 1 mini Crunchie chocolate bars, chopped
- chocolate krispy balls
- chocolate whipped cream
- 5 skinless roasted hazelnuts

Method:
> Place all the ingredients in a blender and mix until well combined.
> While the mixture is blending, melt the melting chocolate and create a hole in the base of the waffle cone. Dip the cone into the melting chocolate and set aside to cool
> Create the chocolate whipped cream by mixing together chocolate syrup with the whipped cream.

Decorate:
> Before pouring the mixture into the glass, create a chocolate rim around the top of the glass (see page 13).
> Pour in the blended mixture until it reaches the bottom of the rim.
> Place the waffle cone on top of glass and place a straw on a diagonal leaning left.
> Place scoop of ice cream in the cone in front of the straw and fill the waffle cone with whipped cream.
> Sit the cone through the straw leaning left and fill cone half way with whipped cream, then crumble mint chocolate over the cream until the cone is filled until the top.

› Staring from the right side of basket cone, create a wave of chocolate chips in direction towards the front of the basket.
› Place one hazelnut in front of each chocolate chip and place the chopped up Crunchie pieces in front of the cone.
› At the front of the waffle basket place two toffees and cover the rest of the whipped cream with chocolate krispy balls.

Chocolate Mania

MC'MAZING

SHAKE INGREDIENTS

- 4 Oreo cookies
- 250g (8oz) mini m&m's

For presentation:
- 1 piccolo glass
- melting chocolate
- 1 long straw
- 1 scoop cone
- sprinkles
- 1 long dessert spoon
- 1 jelly snake
- 2 chocolate Pocky Sticks
- 2 large Oreo cookies
- 1 mini ice cream cone

- 3 scoops vanilla ice cream
- 200ml (7fl oz) milk

- 1 scoop ice cream
- mini m&m's
- 3 Crispy m&m's
- 2 mini Oreo cookies
- 1 tsp caramel syrup
- 1 syrup syringe
- 1 board

Method:

› Place all the ingredients in a blender and mix until well combined.
› While the ingredients are mixing, melt the chocolate and dip your piccolo glass and cone into the chocolate. Also dip your cone into sprinkles before placing both in the fridge to set.

Decorate:

› Once set, fill the glass with the blended mixture until it reaches the bottom of the rim.
› Place a straw and long spoon towards the back of the glass and tie them together using a jelly snake. Give two pumps of caramel syrup to the piccolo glass and then fill the glass with mini m&m's.
› Place two Pokey Sticks in the piccolo glass at the back middle.
› Place half biscuit at the front, right of the glass. Place the ice cream cone on the right side of the piccolo glass.
› Place the ice cream on top of cone and decorate the ice cream with crispy m's and mini Oreos.
› Fill the syrup syringe with caramel syrup and place syringe in front of piccolo and cone.
› Serve immediately and enjoy!

Chocolate Mania
49

TIP: If you're not a fan of the iced chocolate, you can use caramel or strawberry syrup instead!

Chocolate Mania

ICED CHOCOLATE

SHAKE INGREDIENTS

- 3 pumps chocolate syrup
- 1 scoop ice cream
- 300ml (10fl oz) milk

For presentation:
- 1 chocolate dipped and sprinkle covered glass
- 1 long straw
- 4 different candies of your choosing
- whipped cream
- sprinkles

Method:

› Before pouring the mixture into the glass, create a chocolate rim around the top of the glass and top with sprinkles (see page 13).
› Pump three squirts of chocolate syrup around the inside of the glass.
› Place 1 scoop of ice cream neatly into the bottom of the glass and fill the glass up with milk until it reaches the rim.
› Fill remainder with whipped cream tower to about 4–6cm (1.5–2in) high.

Decorate:

› Create your masterpiece! Have fun making nice patterns with the candies of your choice and create a unique iced chocolate.
› Serve immediately and enjoy!

BUENO MARS

SHAKE INGREDIENTS

- 3 Kinder Bueno bar stick
- 2 mini Mars Bars
- 7 frozen raspberries

- 1/2 banana
- 2 scoops vanilla ice cream
- 200ml (7fl oz) milk

For presentation:

- 1 chocolate rimmed glass
- whipped cream
- 1 long straw
- 1 Kinder Bueno stick
- 1 mint sprig
- 1 mini Mars Bar

- 2 skinless hazelnuts
- 5 frozen raspberries
- icing sugar, sifted

Method:
› Place all ingredients in blender and mix until well combined.

Decorate:
› Before pouring the mixture into the glass, create a chocolate rim around the top of the glass (see page 13).
› Pour in the blended mixture until it reaches the base of the glass rim.
› Place a straw at the back, middle of the glass.
› Fill the remaining space in the glass with whipped cream.
› Chop the Kinder Bueno stick in half and place both halves on right hand side of the glass.
› Place the mint sprig on the left side of the straw, making sure that only the leaves are seen.
› Place the mini Mars Bar in front of the mint sprig and place one hazelnut on each side of the Mars Bar. Cover what is left of the whipped cream with frozen raspberries and sprinkle with icing sugar.
› Serve immediately and enjoy!

Chocolate Mania

Chocolate Mania

54

JENGA

SHAKE INGREDIENTS

- 3 Oreo cookies
- 2 white Tim Tams (or white chocolate cookies)
- 1 tbsp Nutella
- 1/2 tbsp peanut butter
- 2 scoops vanilla ice cream
- 200ml (7fl oz) milk

For presentation:
- 1 long straw
- whipped cream
- 1 mint sprig
- 2 Cookies and Cream Kit Kat, broken into sticks (or any cookies and cream flavored chocolate bars)

Method:
> Place all of the shake ingredients in a blender and mix until well combined.

Decorate:
> Pour in the blended mixture until it reaches the base of the glass rim.
> Place a straw in the middle of the glass and fill the remaining space with whipped cream.
> Place two Kit Kat sticks horizontally on edge of jar. Place the next two Kit Kat sticks horizontally the opposite way.
> Repeat the Kit Kat stack two more times, then place the mint sprig in the middle in front of the straw and there you have it, your very own Jenga to drink!
> Serve immediately and enjoy!

TWERK IT

SHAKE INGREDIENTS

- 125g (4oz) ice cubes
- 125ml (4fl oz) milk
- 3 mini Twix sticks

For presentation:
- 1 chocolate covered glass
- 1 long straw
- whipped cream

- 3 tbsp caramel syrup
- pinch of salt
- 1 tsp malt

- 4 original salt flavor crinkle chips
- 1 cube caramel fudge
- 4 orange Smarties
- 1 stem of mint leaves

Method:
> Place all of the shake ingredients into a blender and mix until well combined.

Decorate:
> Before pouring the mixture into the glass, create a chocolate rim around the top of the glass (see page 13).
> Pour the blended mixture into the glass until it reaches the bottom of the rim and then fill the remaining space with whipped cream.
> Place straw in the class towards the back left.
> Create a fan using the chips at the back, right of the straw.
> Chop Twix bar in half and place both pieces on the left, outside of the straw
> Place the mint leaves in front of the straw, between the chips and the Twix.
> Slice the caramel fudge cube and place three small pieces in front of the chips.
> Cover the remaining space with orange Smarties.
> Serve immediately and enjoy!

Chocolate Mania

57

Chocolate Mania
58

COACHELLA

SHAKE INGREDIENTS

- 1 tbsp Nutella
- 1 ½ tbsp coconut oil
- 3 scoops vanilla ice cream
- 200ml milk (7oz)
- 5 lychees (fresh is best otherwise your local supermarket should have tinned)

For presentation:

- 1 chocolate rimmed glass
- 1 long straw
- melting chocolate
- 8 skinless roasted hazelnuts
- 2 Maltesers
- coconut chips
- 1 mini waffle cone
- desiccated coconut
- fresh mint
- whipped cream

Method:

› Place all of the shake ingredients in a blender and mix until well combined.
› While the ingredients are blending, cut 2cm (1in) off the cone, and dip the cone in melted chocolate and desiccated coconut. Leave aside to set.

Decorate:

› Before pouring the mixture into the glass, create a chocolate rim around the top of the glass (see page 13).
› Pour in the blended mixture until it reaches the bottom of the rim of the glass.
› Place a straw in the back, middle of the glass and fill with the remaining space with whipped cream. Place the cone over the straw, sliding the straw through the hole in the cone.
› Fill the cone with fresh mint leaves.
› Place hazelnuts on the edge of the front of the glass and cone and cover the cream with coconut chips.
› Finish off by placing two Maltesers in front of cone, on top of the coconut chips.
› Serve immediately and enjoy!

BILLY BONKA

SHAKE INGREDIENTS

- 3 Oreo cookies
- 2 mini Snickers bar
- 1 tbsp peanut butter

For presentation:
- 2 mini waffles
- 1 chocolate rimmed glass
- 1 long straw
- 7 large twisted pretzels
- 2 large Oreo cookies

- 2 pumps chocolate syrup
- 3 scoops vanilla ice cream
- 200ml (6fl oz) milk

- 4 mini Oreo cookies
- Whipped cream
- handful Reeces pieces

Method:
> Place all of the shake ingredients in a blender and mix until well combined.

Decorate:
> Before pouring the mixture into the glass, create a chocolate rim around the top of the glass (see page 13).
> Pour in the blended mixture until it reaches the bottom of the rim of the glass and fill the remainder of the glass with whipped cream.
> Poke holes through two mini waffles and layer one on top of the glass.
> Cover the waffle with whipped cream, and two opened large Oreo biscuits.
> Top the Oreos with 4 pretzels and a sprinkling of Reeces Pieces.
> Layer on the second mini waffle and top with whipped cream.
> Top the cream with opened mini Oreo cookies and the remaining pretzels.
> Sprinkle with Reeces Pieces.
> Serve immediately and enjoy.

Chocolate Mania
61

SUPER SWEET

- VIVO LA VOGUE -
- BRITTANY'S MUSKETEERS -
- PINK LADY -
- THE HIKE -
- MAYBE IT'S MAPLE -
- FAIRIES DREAM -
- HUBBA HUBBA -
- BANG BANG MERINGUE -
- CREAMING SODA SPIDER -

Super
Sweet

VIVO LA VOGUE

SHAKE INGREDIENTS

- 1 packet creaming soda jelly
- 3 Iced VoVo biscuits
- 1 tsp strawberry jam (jelly)
- 4 marshmallows
- 30ml (1fl oz) vanilla custard
- 3 scoops vanilla ice cream
- 200ml (7fl oz) milk

For presentation:

- 1 chocolate rimmed glass
- 1 long straw
- 1 ½ Iced VoVo
- whipped cream
- 5 mini pink marshmallows
- 5 mini white marshmallows
- 1 tsp strawberry jam
- 1 tsp shredded coconut
- 1 red jelly frog

Method:

- The day before, prepare the creaming soda jelly as per the instructions on the packet. For best results, once the mixture is made, pour 30ml (1fl oz) of the jelly into a chocolate rimmed glass (see page 13) and leave it in the fridge to set overnight.
- The next day, place all of the shake ingredients into a blender and mix until well combined.
- While the shake is blending, cut the Iced VoVo biscuits in to thirds.

Decorate:

- Pour the blended mixture into the jelly filled glass to the bottom of the rim and place a straw at middle, back of the glass.
- Fill the remaining space with whipped cream.
- Place the Iced VoVo pieces on top of the cream on the front and right side of the straw.
- Place mini marshmallows, alternating between white and pink, around the rim of the glass.
- Place the strawberry jam in middle of the shake to cover whipped cream.
- Sprinkle the jam with shredded coconut and top with a red jelly frog.
- Serve immediately and enjoy!

BRITTANY'S MUSKETEERS

SHAKE INGREDIENTS

- 3 musk sticks
- 4 sherbet balls
- 125g (4oz) fairy floss
- 3 scoops lolly bag flavored ice cream
- 200ml (7fl oz) milk

For presentation:
- 1 chocolate rimmed glass
- 1 long straw
- whipped cream
- 1 sherbet lollypop
- 4 sherbet sticks
- fairy floss
- 6 pink musk sticks
- sprinkles

Method:
› Place all the ingredients in a blender and mix until well combined.

Decorate:
› Before pouring the mixture into the glass, create a chocolate rim around the top of the glass (see page 13) and top with sprinkles.
› Pour in the blended mixture until it reaches the bottom of the rim.
› Place a straw on the right side of the shake and fill the remaining space with whipped cream.
› Place a sherbet lollypop inside the straw and place four sherbet sticks to the right of the straw.
› Create a tower with the fairy floss, and create a tower with the musk sticks on top of the shake.
› Serve immediately and enjoy!

Super
Sweet

Super Sweet

PINK LADY

SHAKE INGREDIENTS

- 5 strawberries
- 3 scoops ice cream
- 2 tbsp maple syrup

- 200ml (5fl oz) milk
- 2 teaspoon strawberry syrup

For presentation:
- 1 chocolate rimmed glass
- 1 long straw
- 1 cinnamon donut
- 1 pikelet
- 1 small syrup syringe
- 2 tsp maple syrup

- Pink whipped cream
- 8 strawberries and cream candies
- 1 stem fresh mint
- small handful dessicated coconut
- Icing sugar, sifted

Method:
› Place all the ingredients in a blender and mix until well combined.

Decorate:
› Before pouring the mixture into the glass, create a chocolate rim around the top of the glass and coat with dessicated coconut (see page 13).
› Pour in the blended mixture until it reaches the bottom of the rim.
› Place straw at the back, left of the glass.
› Place the donut on the rim of jar, layer the pikelet on top and cover the top of the pikelet with whipped cream.
› Fill the syrup syringe with maple syrup and place the syringe in the middle of the glass poking into the pikelet.
› Top the pikelet with mint leaves.
› Place the strawberries and cream candies on the rim of the cream creating on top.
› Sprinkle the glass with icing sugar.
› Serve immediately and enjoy!

THE HIKE

SHAKE INGREDIENTS

- 1 pikelet
- 1/2 banana
- 2 ginger kisses
- 1 tbsp maple syrup
- 1 tsp organic chai powder
- 1 tsp honey
- 2 scoops ice vanilla ice cream
- 200ml (7fl oz) milk

For presentation:

- 1 chocolate rimmed glass
- 1 long straw
- 1 pikelet
- Nutella
- 4 round slices fresh banana
- 1 mini chocolate flake, crushed
- handful chocolate krispy balls
- mint leaves

Method:

› Place all the ingredients in a blender and mix until well combined.

› While the ingredients are blending spread Nutella liberally over the pikelet.

Decorate:

› Before pouring the mixture into the glass, create a chocolate rim around the top of the glass (see page 13).

› Pour in the blended mixture until it reaches the bottom of the rim.

› Place the pikelet over the straw, pushing the straw through the pikelet until the pikelet is sitting flat on top of the glass.

› Place the sliced banana around the straw and sprinkle generously with the crushed chocolate flake. Sprinkle with chocolate krispy balls and garnish with min levaes to finish.

› Serve immediately and enjoy!

Super Sweet

Chocolate Mania

72

MAYBE IT'S MAPLE

SHAKE INGREDIENTS

- 2 tsp maple syrup
- 3 scoops vanilla ice cream
- 1 tsp caramel syrup
- 60g (2 oz) pecan
- 100ml (3fl oz) milk

For presentation:
- 1 chocolate rimmed glass
- 1 long straw
- 125g (4 oz) pecans
- 7 edible dried roses
- 1 small pecan pie
- handful chocolate Persian fairy floss
- Crispy chocolate balls
- Icing sugar, to sprinkle
- 1 small empty foil pie shell

Method:
› Place all the ingredients in a blender and mix until well combined.

Decorate:
› Before pouring the mixture into the glass, create a chocolate rim around the top of the glass (see page 13).
› Pour in the blended mixture until it reaches the bottom of the rim, and fill the remainder of the glass with whipped cream.
› Place the straw in the back middle of the glass.
› Place 4 pecans on the edge of the glass towards the front, placing edible dried roses in between.
› Sprinkle with crispy chocolate balls.
› Place the pecan pie on top of the whipped cream and poke a hole through the pie into the glass.
› Place 3 pecans on top of the pie and top with chocolate Persian fairy floss and crispy chocolate balls.
› Cut a hole in the base of the pie shell and place it on top of the glass.
› Feed straw through holes in pie shell and pie.
› Fill the pie shell with chocolate Persian fairy floss, edible dried roses and crispy chocolate balls.
› Dust with icing sugar.
› Serve immediately and enjoy!

Super
Sweet
75

Super
Sweet

FAIRIES DREAM

SHAKE INGREDIENTS

- 4 large Oreo cookies
- 60g (2oz) pink fairy floss
- 125g (4oz) sprinkles
- 1 tsp peach syrup
- 2 scoops vanilla ice cream
- 200ml (7fl oz) milk

For presentation:
- 1 chocolate rimmed glass
- 1 long straw
- whipped cream
- 1 slice white bread buttered
- sprinkles
- 1 musk stick
- 1 large Oreo cookie
- 1 mini Oreo cookie

Method:
› Place all ingredients in a blender and mix until well combined.
› While the shake is mixing butter the bread, cover with sprinkles and cut into triangular slices.

Decorate:
› Before pouring the mixture into the glass, create a chocolate rim around the top of the glass (see page 13).
› Pour in the blended mixture until it reaches the base of the glass rim.
› Place your straw to the left and cover the remaining space with whipped cream.
› From the back of the jar, place one slice of bread in front of the other making sure the tip of the triangle is facing to the right.
› Separate the large Oreo and place the cream side of the cookie on left piece of bread with the other piece slightly in front.
› Separate the mini Oreo and place both chocolate sides one in front of each large Oreo.
› Place the musk stick in the middle of the bread, just behind the two large Oreo cookies and the fairy dream is complete.
› Serve immediately and enjoy!

HUBBA HUBBA

SHAKE INGREDIENTS

- 1 lime Splice ice cream
- 60g (2oz) mixed berries
- 2 pumps lime syrup
- 2 scoops vanilla ice cream
- 200ml (7 fl oz) milk

For presentation:
- 1 chocolate rimmed glass
- 1 long straw
- 2 pieces grape chewing gum
- 2 Froot Loop rings
- 2 Jubes
- 1 candy banana
- 1 small kebab skewer
- whipped cream
- 7 gumballs
- Wonka Nerds

Method:
› Place all the ingredients in a blender and mix until well combined.
› While the ingredients are mixing, layer the candy banana, 2 Froot Loop rings, 1 piece of grape chewing gum (wrapped removed) and Jube onto a small kebab skewer.

Decorate:
› Before pouring the mixture into the glass, create a chocolate rim around the top of the glass (see page 13).
› Pour in the blended mixture until it reaches the bottom of the rim.
› Place straw at the back left of the glass and fill the remaining space with whipped cream.
› Place one piece of grape chewing gum (wrapper on) in front of straw in a diagonal.
› Place your candy skewer on the right side of straw and create a rim at front of shake with the gumballs. Cover the remaining whipped cream with Nerds.
› Serve immediately and enjoy!

Super
Sweet

Super
Sweet
80

BANG BANG MERINGUE

SHAKE INGREDIENTS

- 30ml (1fl oz) passionfruit pulp
- 5 frozen strawberries
- 1 tsp honey
- 200ml (7fl oz) traditional lemonade
- 4 meringue drops
- 6 ice cubes

For presentation:
- 1 glass with sugar rim
- 1 long straw
- 1 meringue nest
- 1 sherbet stick
- 3 strawberry clouds candies
- 3 pink m&m candies
- Persian fairy floss
- 1 sour strawberry strip
- 1 sour bubblegum strip
- sprinkles

Method to make:
› Place all the shake ingredients in a blender and mix until well combined.

Decorate:
› Before pouring the mixture into the glass, create a sugar rim around the top of the glass (see page 13).
› Pour the blended mixture into the glass until it reaches the rim.
› Place the meringue nest on top of the drink and use the straw to create a hole in the meringue nest.
› Place the strawberry clouds on the right hand side of the straw.
› Chop the sherbet stick into 3 pieces and place each piece on the right side of the strawberry clouds. Place of the Persian fairy floss in middle, then place 3 pink m&m candies on left side of the fairy floss. Wrap the sour strawberry strip around the straw and then use the sour bubblegum strip to tie a knot to hold together the strawberry sour strap and the straw.
› Finish off by adding sprinkles over the top of the drink.
› Serve immediately and enjoy!

CREAMING SODA SPIDER

SHAKE INGREDIENTS

- 1 sugar rimmed glass
- 1 long straw
- strawberry syrup
- 1 scoop vanilla ice cream
- 1 can creaming soda
- 2 red jelly snake
- 3 strawberries and cream jelly candies
- 2 red jelly frogs
- 2 red Gummi Bears
- sprinkles

Method:
- Before pouring the mixture into the glass, create a sugar rim around the top of the glass (see page 13).
- Pour the strawberry syrup around the inside of the glass (the more you use, the stronger the taste!).
- Place a scoop of ice cream into the bottom and then throw in all of the candies.
- Finish with a topping of sprinkles.
- Finish with sprinkles.
- Pour in the creaming soda.
- Serve with a spoon and a straw.
- Serve immediately and enjoy!

Super
Sweet
83

CRAZY COOL

- INFAMOUS NUTELLA MILKSHAKE
- CUSTARTED
- INFAMOUS PEANUT BUTTER MILKSHAKE
- WHEEL OF FORTUNE
- FIFI'S FAIRY TALE
- TVC TREE
- MY KIND OF KOOL
- TERRY AND SUE

Crazy Cool

INFAMOUS NUTELLA MILKSHAKE

SHAKE INGREDIENTS

- 1 scoop vanilla ice cream
- 3 tsp Nutella
- 1 pump chocolate syrup
- 200ml (7fl oz) milk

For presentation:
- 1 chocolate rimmed glass
- 1 long straw
- whipped cream
- 7 sour worms
- 7 hazelnuts (skinless and roasted)
- ½ licorice all sorts
- 1 mini wafer cone
- 2 pieces of colored popcorn
- dusting chocolate powder
- whipped cream (to fill ¼ jar)

Method:
- Place all the ingredients into a blender and mix until well combined.
- While the ingredients are blending, cut the end of the wafer cone and dip it into melted chocolate then sprinkles.

Decorate:
- Before pouring the mixture into the glass, create a chocolate rim around the top of the glass (see page 13).
- Pour the blended mixture into the glass until it is about 2cm (1in) away from the rim.
- Place a straw at the back of the glass and fill the remaining space with whipped cream.
- Place the cut and chocolate dipped cone over the straw.
- Scatter the hazelnuts around the rim of the glass.
- Place the sliced licorice pieces in front of the cone.
- Place the colored popcorn inside the cone and then fill cone with sour worms.
- Sprinkle the finished drink with chocolate powder to just lightly cover the decoration.
- Serve immediately and enjoy!

CUSTARTED

SHAKE INGREDIENTS

- 5 cubes mango
- 60ml (2fl oz) vanilla custard
- 5 chocolate Tim Tams
- 2 tbsp Milo
- 1 tbsp organic coconut oil
- 2 scoops vanilla ice cream
- 200ml (7fl oz) milk

For presentation:

- 1 chocolate sprinkle dipped glass
- 1 long straw
- sprinkles
- 1 waffle basket
- 2 scoops vanilla ice cream
- whipped cream
- 1 mini chocolate waffle
- yellow Persian fairy floss
- 3 mini chocolate Tim Tams
- 1 tbsp Milo
- 60g (2oz) chocolate krispy balls
- 1 Tim Tam, crushed
- melting chocolate
- 1 mini meringue nest

Method:

› Place all ingredients in a blender jug, and mix until well combined.

› While the ingredients are blending, heat up the melting chocolate and cut a hole in the waffle basket.

› Dip your waffle and the tip of the meringue nest into melted chocolate and then into the sprinkles. Leave both aside to set.

Decorate:

› Before pouring the mixture into the glass, create a chocolate rim around the top of the glass and roll the glass in sprinkles (see p. 13).

› Pour in the blended mixture until it reaches the bottom of the rim.

› Place the waffle basket on top of the glass and slide the straw through the hole.

› Put two scoops of ice cream in front of the straw and fill the remainder of the waffle basket with whipped cream.

› Slide the chocolate waffle through the straw and then place a layer of fairy floss on top of the chocolate waffle.

› Spike your meringue through the straw and place three mini Tim Tams at the front of the waffle basket.

› Cover the remainder of the shake with whipped cream, sprinkles, Milo, chocolate krispy balls and crushed up Tim Tam to finish.

› Serve immediately and enjoy!

Crazy Cool
89

Crazy
Cool

INFAMOUS PEANUT BUTTER MILKSHAKE

SHAKE INGREDIENTS

- 3 tsp smooth peanut butter
- 1 pump caramel syrup
- 1 pump chocolate syrup

- 1 scoop vanilla ice cream
- 200ml (7fl oz) milk

For presentation:

- 1 mini cone
- 6 sour coke bottles
- 15 peanut bite Reeses Pieces
- 1 colored popcorn

- dusting of chocolate powder
- whipped cream (to fill ¼ jar)

Method:

- Place all ingredients in a blender and mix until well combined.
- While the ingredients are mixing cut the bottom off the mini cone, dip it in chocolate and sprinkles and set aside.

Decorate:

- Before pouring the mixture into the glass, create a chocolate rim around the top of the glass (see page 13)
- Pour the blended mixture into the glass until it reaches the bottom of the rim.
- Place a straw in the shake, towards the back of the glass.
- Fill the rest of the jar with whipped cream.
- Place the cone on the straw topside up, and fill the cone with colored popcorn.
- Cover the whipped cream with Reese's Pieces.
- Place the sour coke bottles inside the cone and finish with a small dusting of chocolate powder.
- Serve immediately and enjoy!

WHEEL OF FORTUNE

SHAKE INGREDIENTS

- 1 large Wagon Wheel
- 6 large marshmallows
- 2 tbsp strawberry jam
- 1 tbsp peanut butter
- 3 scoops vanilla ice cream
- 200ml (7fl oz) milk

For presentation:
- 1 chocolate rimmed glass
- 1 long straw
- whipped cream
- 1 small Wagon Wheel
- 6 white mini marshmallows
- chocolate krispy balls
- 1 mini chocolate Flake bar, crushed

Method:
- Place all the ingredients in a blender and mix until well combined.
- While the ingredients are blending, slice the small Wagon Wheel into quarters and set aside.

Decorate:
- Before pouring the mixture into the glass, create a chocolate rim around the top of the glass (see page 13).
- Pour in the blended mixture until it reaches the bottom of the rim. Fill the remainder of the jar with whipped cream.
- Place your Wagon Wheel quarters on the right side of glass creating a fan.
- On the left side of the glass, scatter the mini marshmallows and chocolate krispy balls.
- Sprinkle the crushed chocolate Flake bar over the shake to finish.
- Serve immediately and enjoy!

Crazy
Cool
93

Crazy
Cool
94

FIFI'S FAIRY TALE

SHAKE INGREDIENTS

- 3 mini Crunchie chocolate bars
- 2 tbsp caramel fudge

For presentation:
- 1 chocolate rimmed glass
- 1 long straw
- 1 cinnamon donut
- whipped cream
- small handful of white Persian fairy floss

- 2 chocolate chip cookies
- pinch of salt
- 200 ml milk

- 2 Pocky stick, green tea flavored
- fresh flowers (your choice)
- dried rose petals

Method:
› Place all the ingredients in a blender and mix until well combined.

Decorate:
› Before pouring the mixture into the glass, create a chocolate rim around the top of the glass (see page 13).
› Pour in the blended mixture until it reaches halfway the bottom of the rim.
› Place the cinnamon donut on top of the glass and put the straw through the middle of the donut, into the shake.
› Cover donut with whipped cream and white Persian fairy floss.
› Place the Pocky sticks on left side of straw and layer the glass with fresh flowers.
› Sprinkle the shake with dried rose petals.
› Serve immediately and enjoy!

TVC TREE

SHAKE INGREDIENTS

- 4 Mars Bars
- 2 Oreo cookies
- 1 tbsp malt
- 25ml vanilla custard (0.8oz)
- 7 ice cubes
- 1 tbsp Nutella
- 200ml (7fl oz) milk

For presentation:
- 1 chocolate rimmed glass
- 1 long straw
- whipped cream
- green dye
- 3 chocolate gold coins
- 1 mini waffle cone
- gold tinsel
- red crispy m&ms
- Maltesers
- chocolate star
- icing sugar, sifted

Method:
› Place all the ingredients in a blender and mix until well combined.
› While the ingredients are blending, mix together the whipped cream with green food dye.

Decorate:
› Before pouring the mixture into the glass, create a chocolate rim around the top of the glass (see page 13).
› Pour in the blended mixture until it reaches the bottom of the rim.
› Fill rest of glass with plain whipped cream and place the three gold coins around the glass.
› Place the mini cone upside down on top of the drink, in the middle of the gold coins.
› Use the green whipped cream to cover the cone in circular motions.
› Decorate the cone using the red crispy m&ms and Maltesers.
› Place the chocolate star on top of cone and dust your tree with icing sugar.
› Serve immediately and enjoy!

Crazy
Cool
97

Crazy Cool

MY KIND OF KOOL

SHAKE INGREDIENTS

- 1 packet Kinder Bueno
- 2 Kinder chocolate bars
- 1 tbsp Nutella
- 2 pumps chocolate syrup
- 3 scoops vanilla ice cream
- 200ml (7fl oz) milk

For presentation:
- 1 chocolate rimmed glass
- 1 long straw
- whipped cream
- ½ Kinder Surprise Egg
- ½ Kinder Bueno bar
- 1 small piece of Kinder chocolate bar
- 5 skinless roasted hazelnuts
- 3 Maltesers
- 1 chocolate flake, crushed

Method:
› Place all the ingredients in a blender and mix until well combined.

Decorate:
› Before pouring the mixture into the glass, create a chocolate rim around the top of the glass (see page 13)
› Pour in the blended mixture until it reaches the bottom of the rim.
› Place a straw at back towards the left of the glass.
› Fill remaining space in the glass with whipped cream until it reaches the top of the rim.
› Place half of the Kinder Surprise Egg on the right, front side of straw.
› On the left side of straw, place the Kinder chocolate bar, and the Kinder Bueno slight in front of it.
› Create a rim of skinless roasted hazelnuts from the Kinder Bueno bar to the Kinder Surprise Egg.
› Place three Maltesers inside the Kinder Surprise Egg and finish by sprinkling the crushed chocolate flake over the drink.
› Serve immediately and enjoy!

TERRY AND SUE

SHAKE INGREDIENTS

- whipped cream
- 2 sponge fingers
- 100ml (3fl oz) milk
- 1 tsp coffee
- 3 Maltesers
- icing sugar, sifted

For presentation:
- 1 chocolate rimmed glass
- 1 long straw
- 1 plastic food syringe
- 1 long dessert spoon

Method:
- Chop the sponge fingers in half and place into the chocolate rimmed glass.
- Place a long spoon and straw into the glass and pour in the milk.

Decorate:
- Fill the syringe with coffee.
- Place a small amount of whipped cream and Maltesers into a small bowl.
- Place the glass, bowl and syringe onto a serving board to serve.
- Serve immediately and enjoy!

Crazy
Cool
103

GLOSSARY OF TREATS

While some of these treats can be difficult to find, all can be found in international supermarkets, or sweets stores.

Iced VoVo – Similar to a Mikado biscuit in the UK, this treat is a biscuit (cookie) layered with marshallows, strawberry jam and desiccated coconut

Maltesers – Maltesers are small chocolate balls filled with a malt honeycomb center.

Flake – Flakes are a thin chocolate bar made up of thin layers of rolled chocolate.

Tim Tam – Tim Tams are a popular chocolate biscuit (cookie) made of two layers of chocolate biscuit (cookie) separated by a light chocolate cream filling and coated in chocolate.

Oreo – Oreos are a sandwich cookie consisting of two chocolate cookies with a sweet crème filling.

Crunchie – A chocolate bar filled with honeycomb toffee sugar.

Jubes – A jelly candy coated in sugar.

Milky Way – Similar to a Mars Bar, a Milky Way is made of chocolate malt nougat, coated with caramel and chocolate.

Nutella – A hazelnut spread, commonly found in all supermarkets.

Strawberry Clouds – a red, cloud shaped soft candy, strawberry flavored.

Sour Strips (strawberry and bubblegum) – strips of sour and gummy strawberry or bubblegum flavored candy.

Kinder Bueno – a light chocolate bar with a creamy hazelnut center and crispy wafer coated in chocolate.

Kinder Surprise Egg – a small, hollow chocolate egg filled with a small toy.

Mamee noodles – hardened, squiggly strips, condensed into a tight, square block and are designed to be eaten as is.

Ovalteenies – Ovalteenies are round sweets made of compressed Ovaltine, which is a chocolate milk flavoring product made from malt extract.

Pocky Sticks – A popular Japanese snack food that can be bought in supermarkets. Pocky Sticks are chocolate coated biscuit sticks.

Sour Worms – A small gummy candy shaped like a worm. Often come in bright colors and are coated in sugar.

Rice Bubbles (Rice Krispies) – a popular cereal made from crisped rice.

Reese's Pieces – a peanut butter candy, colored orange, yellow and brown.

Strawberries and Cream – a small gummi candy with a white base and red top, to look like a strawberry on top of cream.

Gummi Bears – a small fruit gum candy, similar to jelly babies.

Musk Stick – a small semi-soft pink stick with a musk taste and smell.

Banana lollies (candies) – a small, yellow banana shaped candies. Can be bought from candy stores.

Jersey Caramels –a small, square shaped caramel flavored candy.

Monte Carlo – a sweet biscuit (cookie) made of golden syrup, honey and coconut biscuits (cookies) and filled with vanilla cream and raspberry jam.

Ginger Kisses – a sweet ginger cookie filled with butter cream.

Milo – a chocolate and malt powder to be mixed with milk or water to create a chocolate drink.

Wagon Wheels – a sweet sandwich cookie filled with marshmallow and coated in chocolate.

INDEX

B
Bang Bang Meringue 80
Billy Bonka 60
Brittany's Musketeers 66
Bueno Mars 52

C
Chainana 22
Chocolate milkshake 34
Coachella 58
Creaming Soda Spider 82
Crunchie Kisses 32
Custarted 88

D
Decorating your glass 13
Double Decker 44

F
Fairies Dream 76
Fifi's Fairy Tale 94

G
Glossary 108

H
Hubba Hubba 78

I
Iced chocolate 50
Infamous Nutella Milkshake 86
Infamous Peanut Butter Milkshake 90

J
Jenga 54

M
Magic doodle 42
Malt my heart 36
Man-go-crazy 24
Maybe it's Maple 74
Mc'Mazing 48
Mixed berry smoothie 28
Mocha Madness 38
My Kind of Kool 100

N
Notes about safety 11

P
Pash me 18
Peach as bro 16
Peachy mango 20
Pina colada 26
Pink Lady 68

S
Salty Knickers 40

T
Terry and Sue 102
The Hike 70
TVC Tree 96
Twerk it 56

V
Viva la Vogue 64

W
Wheel of Fortune 92

ACKNOWLEDGEMENTS

Thank you from Matthew, Sarah and Brendan to all our loyal customers and followers for being a part of The Vogue Café's Decadent Shake journey. Your support makes the café what it is and gives us this great and wonderful opportunity of making a book which we can share with you.

Big shout out to Marcel, Big Pappa, Lynette, Big Mumma for the endless and unconditional support they provide. Our partners – Natasha, Omer and Emma for always pushing us to be creative. Our siblings Kristen and George for being our taste testers, and our awesome little kids, who we can't wait to teach all the tricks! To our wonderful and awesome staff, who we really do consider to be apart of our family, thank you for coming to work and giving it your all day in and day out.

AUTHOR BIO

Matthew, Sarah and Brendan Aouad are siblings running a family business making the world a happier place one decadent shake at a time. With experience from every facet of a business, each sibling brings an innovative flair to how a small business should be run and shakes should be made, creating a sweet rivalry that has turned into some of their finest decadent shakes time after time. Love life!

First published in 2016.
This paperback edition first published in 2018 by New Holland Publishers
London • Sydney • Auckland

131–151 Great Titchfield Street, London W1W 5BB, United Kingdom
1/66 Gibbes Street, Chatswood, NSW 2067, Australia
5/39 Woodside Ave, Northcote, Auckland 0627, New Zealand

www.newhollandpublishers.com

Copyright © 2018 New Holland Publishers Copyright © 2018 in text:
Matthew Aouad, Sarah Aouad, Brendan Aouad
Copyright © 2018 in images: New Holland Publishers, Shutterstock

All rights reserved. No part of this publication may be reproduced, stored in a retrieval system or transmitted, in any form or by any means, electronic, mechanical, photocopying, recording or otherwise, without the prior written permission of the publishers and copyright holders.

A record of this book is held at the British Library and the National Library of Australia.

ISBN 9781760790004

Group Managing Director: Fiona Schultz
Publisher: Diane Ward
Project Editor: Kaitlyn Smith
Designer: Sara Lindberg
Photographer: Sue Stubbs
Production Director: James Mills-Hicks
Printer: Times International Printing, Malaysia

10 9 8 7 6 5 4 3 2 1

Keep up with New Holland Publishers on Facebook
www.facebook.com/NewHollandPublishers